Waterfalls of Therapy

Michael R. Elliott, PhD

~ Poetry, Healing, & Growth Series ~

www.universityprofessorspress.com

Book Copyright © 2019. University Professors Press.

The author retains the copyright of all the individual poems.

Waterfalls of Therapy
By Michael R. Elliott

All rights reserved. No portion of this book may be reproduced, by any process or technique, without the express written consent of the publisher.

    ISBN-13: 978-1-939686-46-6
    ISBN-10: 1-939686-46-6

University Professors Press
Colorado Springs, CO

Cover Design by Laura Ross
Cover Photo by Eadie Elliott
All Interior Photos by Eadie Elliott

Poetry, Healing, and Growth Series

Stay Awhile: Poetic Narratives on Multiculturalism and Diversity
Louis Hoffman & Nathaniel Granger, Jr. (Eds.)

Capturing Shadows: Poetic Encounters Along the Path of Grief and Loss
Louis Hoffman & Michael Moats (Eds.)

Journey of the Wounded Soul: Poetic Companions for Spiritual Struggles
Louis Hoffman & Steve Fehl (Eds.)

Our Last Walk: Using Poetry for Grieving and Remembering Our Pets
Louis Hoffman, Michael Moats, and Tom Greening (Eds.)

Poems For and About Elders (Revised & Expanded Edition)
Tom Greening

Connoisseurs of Suffering: Poetry for the Journey to Meaning
Jason Dias & Louis Hoffman (Eds.)

Silent Screams: Poetic Journeys Through Addiction & Recovery
Nathaniel Granger, Jr., & Louis Hoffman

Waterfalls of Therapy
Michael R. Elliott

Poetry, Healing, and Growth Series

The ancient healing art of poetry has been used across cultures for thousands of years. In the Poetry, Healing, and Growth book series, the healing and growth-facilitating nature of poetry is explored in depth through books of poetry and scholarship, as well as through practical guides on how to use poetry in the service of healing and growth. Poetry written with an intention to transform suffering into an artistic encounter is often different in process and style from poetry written for art's sake. This series offers engagement with the poetic greats and literary approaches to poetry while also embracing the beauty of fresh, poetic starts and encouraging readers to embark upon their own journey with poetry. Whether you are an advanced poet, avid consumer, or novice to poetry, we are confident you will find something to inspire your thinking on your personal path toward healing and growth.

Series Editors,
Carol Barrett, PhD; Steve Fehl, PsyD; Nathaniel Granger, Jr, PsyD; Tom Greening, PhD; and Louis Hoffman, PhD

Table of Contents

Foreword by Paul Jurkowski   i
Preface   iii

Part I: Beginnings   1
What Brings You Here   3
Beginning   4
What Did It Begin   5
I Want To Be Here Don't I   6
What to Do   7
Am I Okay   8
When Will I Know Me   9
Business as Usual   10
Where You Are   11
Pain   12
Pathology and Communication   13
Ready to See My Hurt   14
The One   15
One More Time   16
A Beginning   17

Part II: Confusion   19
Way, Style, and Pattern of Living   21
This Therapy or Prejudice   22
Confusion   23
I Am Empty   24
Loggerheads   25
Untwisting   26
Truth Enough   27
How Soon Will I Be Okay   28

Part III: Process   29
Where Am I Hidden   31
Knowledge Resolves   32
I Just Talk with People   33
Down Under   34
Every Time   35

Picker of Nits	36
The Smallest Point	37
A Picker of Nits Two	38
Mostly the Words Play	39
Unstuck	40
Interlocked	41
The Responsibility of Living or How Long Does This Go On	42
Staccato	43
Pontification	44
Part IV: Approaches to Therapy	45
DSM	47
Patient Client	48
Doing Therapy with Yourself	49
Follow the Client	50
How do You Come to That	51
Therapy is Mundane	52
Part V: Change	53
What is Wrong with Me	55
Therapy is About Change	56
Seeing	57
Part VI: Self	59
Hope	61
I Am	62
Understand	63
The Things I Don't Like	64
In the Name of Now	65
Happy	66
Fears	67
Everything Me	68
I Am the One I Seek	69
My Safe Place	70
Part VII: Relationship	71
If You Let Them Go	73
It is Difficult for Us	74
What is Going On	75
It's All About Me	76
He Used to Love Me	77

Don't You Understand	78
A Common Claim	79

Part VIII: Being Okay — 81
Crazy	83
Empty of Hurt	84
Incomplete	85
The End of Therapy	86

Part IX: The Therapist — 87
In the First Years of the Therapist	89
Time for Therapy	90
Therapy Timeout	91
Stillness	92
Mentor	93
Turn It Around	94
Trust the Doctor	95
Termination	96
So	97
In a Flash	98
Me	99

Part X: Outcomes — 101
If I Go Forward What	103
Change	104
Moment	105
Present or Hi	106
Empty of Hurt	107
It Seen or the It of Things	108
Mostly the Words Play	109
I Can	110
The Waterfall	111

Foreword

Don Miguel Ruiz says, in *Prayers*, "Everyone creates his or her own story; everyone lives in their own dream. To recover awareness is to see life the way it is, not the way we want it to be." He feels that this dream we live in keeps us from finding true love for ourselves and others, from seeing the truth of creation.

In a way, when people come to a therapist for help, they bring the dream and the truth, and, unfortunately, the therapist often brings not only the truth, but their own dreams. I imagined it like this: Someone seeking help from you is like the sun shining through the leaves and branches of a tree outside your window—and your window represents your perceptions. The sun is the truth of existence—the power of creation and the love inherent in our existence, but the tree, *and* your window, are dreams that can cloud the truth.

I've known Michael for somewhere around 15 years, or, more truthfully, I've been his friend for 15 years—he is, like all of us, not fully knowable. He possesses the rare gift of desire to see clearly, and he has been polishing his window, lovingly removing as much judgment and preconception as he can for many years as a therapist. What has resulted is a window that almost disappears, and the interplay of light and shadow that enters the room with him is seen more clearly.

This book is the poetry inherent in that loving task, and the images are magically caught by the words on these pages like images on photographic plates.

I truly love Michael, and he is a gift to our world, in great part because he has created a window that is a window into the soul.

~ Paul Jurkowski

Preface

Some of these pieces are about the feelings of the therapist, some about the feelings of the client, some about both. Some are about how being a therapist has influenced my view of the world. All are about the influence that comes from being a therapist. I could have written none of these pieces other than through being a therapist.

This small collection of verse is written as a personal response to having concluded a quarter century of providing psychotherapy. It is written from several perspectives. First, it is written from the perspective of counseling being a very simple dialogical enterprise. The presumption of this model of therapy is that the therapeutic exercise is nothing more than one person seeking the help of another in sorting out the thoughts and feelings that stand in the way of resolving intrapersonal conflict and struggle. The role of the therapist is to raise questions that ask the client to engage in the process of clarification and resolution of confusions, contradictions, and uncertainties in their life. This is largely done by encouraging the client to look at how they enter into the process of confusion, contradiction, and uncertainty. Second, it is written from the perspective of having learned the learnings implied or explicit in this volume from either my mentor or from my clients. The collection is a tribute to both. Third, it is written from the point of view that the reader can ascertain the speaker in the verses without being told. The exercise of discerning the speaker is helpful in understanding the intent of the verse. It also enhances and amplifies seeing the working of the dialogic process. It is my hope these musings will encourage you to take a look at yourself more intently and with greater resolution than you have in the past no matter how well you currently do so. I have been working at this with myself for approximately the last fifty years and have not even come close to running out of material. If you have completed the process, please get in touch with me and let me know how you have succeeded in doing so.

With love,
Michael Elliott

Part I: Beginnings

Photo by Eadie Elliott

What Brings You Here

So, what brings you here
Me
Yes, WHAT about you brings you here
Oh, I see. I don't know
So, why are you here then
I need to be here
I see
Let's continue

Beginning

So
Where shall we begin
Begin what
Begin our talk
Oh
At the beginning
Where is that
Where is it for you
It is kind of where I first thought of coming here
And where were you then
Confused
Seems I've been that way most of my life
At least ever since high school
Okay let's start there
Let's start with in what way you have been confused ever since
high school
Well, I didn't belong
Belong how
We have begun haven't we
Yes

When Did It Begin

So when did the trouble start
What do you mean
When did it begin
Long long ago
In a place far far away
Oh
I mean your struggle
What struggle
The one that began long long ago in a place far far away
Oh that
Well when I was sure my parents were going to go away
Okay let's start there and then

I Want to Be Here Don't I

I want to be here don't I
I show up
But I am not here
I am stuck
Afraid
Alone
Vulnerable
I can't let anyone know any of this
Because if I do
What will he think of me
And if I don't what will I think
I think
I will start here for now
Better start somewhere
Better to not be stuck
Can be afraid
Better to not be alone
I can be vulnerable
I can let someone know

What to Do

So what to do
To move
To let go
To be different
To be me
To open
To examine
To explore
To share
To show
To learn to know
To cease to hide
To cease to blame
To be
Is what to do

Am I Okay

I am sure I am not okay
I want to be okay
Okay
I really do
Are you not okay
Yes
How so?
I don't know
How can you know you are not ok if you don't know how you are not okay
I am not sure
Not sure how
Not sure how I know
Do you know
I am not sure
Good
That is a starting place

When Will I Know Me

When will I know me
When I am here
When I am open
When I am transparent
When I feel safe to look in
When I look
When I see
Then I will know me
Bit by bit
Piece by piece
Unraveling
Unfolding
Seeing as things are
I will know me

Business as Usual

Here we go again
The company cheats
The press speaks
Nothing really changes
The ethic
The moral
The life view
Get something for nothing
Stretch it
Nudge it
Get some advantage
Make it for less
Shave the points
Business as usual
And you ask what brings me to therapy

Where You Are

I don't know where to start
Start where you are
Where am I
Where are you
I am in a fearful place
Start there
Start
Begin
Deal with you
Begin to open
Begin to see
Begin to understand
But I am afraid
Yes,
You have begun

Pain

When did it begin
A long time ago
When was a long time ago
When it started
When did it start
I don't remember
How do you know it began when you don't remember the beginning
It feels like a part of who I am
What part
The part I do not like
What don't you like about it
The pain
How does it hurt
Like guilt
Did you do anything wrong
I don't think so
Would you know
I think so
So
You're not guilty
No
So that is the way it is

Pathology and Communication

I think I am really mixed up
Well, let's talk about it
But I can't because I am mixed up
What I say will be mixed up
Well, you can tell me about your mix up
I can listen
And I am not mixed up
At least not in the same way as you
So I won't be mixed up about what you say about your mix up
And I can ask you some questions about your mix up
And you can tell me if what I say seems to fit
I like you
I like you too
That's not mixed up
We must be making progress

Ready to See My Hurt

I am so filled with mixed upness
I confuse things for the sake of being confused
I distort things so I may not see
I am prejudice so that I may not know
I hide so that I may not be seen
I am silent so that I may not be known
I blame so that I may not suffer
I lie so that I may appear honest
I make noise so I will not be heard
If I am heard
I may be known
If I am known
I may see my hurt
If I see my hurt I may die
If I see my hurt I may know that I lived
I want to live
I am ready to see my hurt
I will not die until my time

The One

The patient
The client
The person
The one on the couch
The one speaking
The one listening
The one changing
The one opening
The one discovering
The one becoming at one with herself
The one beginning to know
The one growing
The one gaining clarity
The one less afraid
The one asking
The one answering
The one discovering her own peace
The one beginning to move effortlessly
The one with consistency
The one
One
You
All of us

One More Time

We come together
We continue one more time
The one looking
The other being shown
The other a guest
In the mind of the one
The other pointing at the haze
Then the one seeing as it lifts
Having seen moving on
Another piece
Another element
Another part
The parts of the whole
They begin to emerge

A Beginning

The worst of times
The best
To see the face of change
To be change
To awaken
To be alert
To be clear
The confusion has lifted
I can see
I am no longer alone
Thanks for being willing
Now I can live
Now I can be in relation to the universe
Now I see I am part of all things

Part II: Confusion

Photo by Eadie Elliott

Way, Style, and Pattern of Living

At first just an inconvenience
That is,
My confusion
My uncertainty
My contradiction
Then it blends some
It repeats itself
It sort of gets fixed
It is the way I think
It becomes more my style of living
It becomes more the pattern of my life
The way style and pattern of my life
That leave me in a mess

This Therapy or Prejudice

This therapy
This therapy stuff is not real
Strong people just get on and get over it
It is for weak people
It makes them weaker
Life either kills you or makes you tougher
Babysitters
Of
Lollygaggers
Therapists are worthless
I myself
I am strong
I know what I see
And I call a spade a spade
I have it all together
I am together and have it all

Confusion

This looks like that
But it cannot be
Because that is not this
I have mixed it up
This is this
And
That is that
I kissed her
She must love me
No
She kissed me
I must love her
No
I kissed her
It was pleasurable
Yes
No more confusion
A kiss does not equal love
A kiss equals pleasure

I Am Empty

How do you know you are empty
I feel nothing
Yet you feel
Yes but nothing
Is Feeling nothing something
Yes
What is the something you feel
I don't feel anything
You just said you feel nothing
What is this nothing
I don't know
Well, good
At least now you know it is something you don't know
And that feeling nothing is something
You can find the something that is nothing
Tell me about this emptiness

Loggerheads

You said…
No I didn't
Well, that is what you said
But I didn't mean that
It sounded like you did
Are you sure
Well, I don't know
I am confused now
How
Well, I thought therapy was supposed to help me resolve
confusion
Not create it

Untwisting

How can I untwist things
What things and in what way twisted
Well, you know the things that cause me trouble
Okay, so we will talk of things that cause you trouble
So tell me in what way twisted
Well, mixed up
Mixed up?
Yes, things not where they belong in my head
How so?
Well, I think stupid things
Okay I get it
Thinking stupid things is being mixed up
Hey you are pretty clever
No, I think you figured that all out yourself
I just told you what you told me you had figured out
You are pretty clever

Truth Enough

What part plays truth
True to what standard
True to whom
Is invention not truth
Is not fiction truth
Is the patient not his own truth
No matter how perplexed
So what does he have to be
To be okay
Honest
Truthful
Or is open enough
Does open require
Honesty
Or truthfulness
With self
With others
By what definition
To what standard
If I know how I am
Is that not enough

How Soon Will I Be Okay

Will I be okay soon
I don't know
You're the doctor
You should know
Well, I don't
Are you not okay
I don't know
Then how do you come to ask how soon you will be okay
Can I trust you
Yes
How do I know
I don't know
Then how can I know
Tell me how you can know
You will know when you trust me
I want to trust you
Good
I want to be okay
Does that make it so
No
Then where to begin
Where do you want to begin
Well, you said wanting would not make it so
It will in this case
Because one place is as good as the next
How soon will I be okay

Part III:
Process

Photo by Eadie Elliott

Where Am I Hidden

Where am I hidden
In the confusion
In the contradiction
In the uncertainty
In the shame
In the doubt
In the fear
In the lies
In the darkness of my mind
I seek to be known
I want to know me
I want to know
I want
I work
I know
I remove my hiding places
There are no hiding places
I am no longer hidden
I no longer hide

Knowledge Resolves

The source of all knowledge is self
Knowledge is awareness
Awareness comes from attentiveness
Attentiveness comes
At the cost of quietness
Quietness is born of active alertness
As the person begins to listen to himself
Then the mystery begins to subside
The confusion begins to resolve
The contradictions are seen for what they are
Action born of being mixed up
Holding forth
With things that fail to abide with one another
Truth tellers lying
Liars truth telling
Shame proclaiming no guilt
Sadness proclaiming happiness
Anger proclaiming love
These I begin to see
As I begin to listen
As I begin to see myself
As I am leaving madness
I
Behind

I Just Talk with People

I don't do anything
I just talk with people
Oh, Yes
I listen
I ask
I follow
I seek to know
I look for what is left out
I encourage people to fill in
I look for the whole
I look for the confusions
I look for the distortions
I look for where the picture is incomplete
I engage
I open up what is closed
Or left unopen
I just talk with people

Down Under

I feel down under the world
I feel like crap
I feel horrible
Well, which is it
Under, crap or horrible
All of them
Then where shall we start
Down under the world
Like the weight of everything is on me
And you are responsible for everything
Well no but I feel that way
Like you are responsible
No, like someone thinks I am
Who might be doing that thinking
I don't know
Then how do you know it is like someone thinks so
Well, it use to feel that way when my mom said you had better do it right
So, could that be it
A feeling from the past
It sure feels like it
Is that the crap
Is it
It could be
It feels like it
And what about the horrible

Every Time

Every time I see it
I get very frightened
I begin to sweat
I begin to shake
And what if you didn't get frightened
But I do
I know but what if you didn't
Well that would be the end of it
So if you wouldn't be frightened when you see it you wouldn't
sweat or shake
Yes
So all you have to do is not be frightened
Yes
And you just thought of not being frightened a moment ago
Yes
Does thinking something is frightening make it so
Yes
So what about thinking something is not frightening
Just thinking it
(Because you and I know it is really frightening)
Would that make it so

Picker of Nits

Every time I give you an answer
You ask another question
Or make a comment that might as well be a question
Every time I ask a question
You give an answer that might as well be a question
Until it is over no matter where I end up
You have a question about that
Just when I think I have settled it
You ask me about it
And there we go
What is the it
Well, are you okay with that
Well, I keep coming back don't I
You know
I have finally figured something out
Yes, what's that
You are a picker of nits
That's what you do
Yes, I guess so
What went on with you to figure that out
I picked the nit

The Smallest Point

It started somewhere
It was the smallest point
I couldn't see it
I had to feel it
It was there
I knew it was there
It kept getting in my way
I would trip on it
It was in the past
Always the past present
That is
Where it started
That was it
It started where it started
Way back
A piece of fear
Or was it shame
Shamefully fearful
Perhaps
Yes, that was it
It is gone now
I don't trip on it any more

A Picker of Nits Two

Did you mean to do that
Well, I did it
But did you intend to
I must have
It was me who did it
But do you recall if you chose to do it
I recall
What
Doing it
And how did it come from you
What do you mean
Literally, how did you do it
What was the process
You mean was I angry
I don't know
Was that it
Did you act out of anger
What was the source of the act
I was hurt
There it is
You acted out of hurt
Why didn't you just tell me that
I didn't know
Until you told me

Mostly the Words Play

When the sessions go well
They are less work and more play
A bantering among themselves
The words go on
Effortlessly
Without any trying
One idea
Jumps off the next
The two come together
They blend and make sense
Then the next idea emerges
It fits too
It is as though I do not have to try
I simply see more of what was hidden
Simply I see more
I see simply
Without seeming
Just being
Flowing
Listening
Understanding

Unstuck

Notice how the words get jammed together
That is notice how they stick and get stuck
Yet notice how they pry themselves loose
How they begin to flow a little bit here and there
Notice how the words clean up their act
Almost on their own
But by your effort
By your seeking
By your attempt to understand
You are less stuck than you were
You are somewhat unstuck
Continue on
It will open even more
It will flow
More easily

Interlocked

It is better now
It is all the stuff that was mixed up
It would be better to call it its
There were so many things
I could not work them out
They were jumbled
Not clear
Interlocked
Now I can take them one at a time
I can open them up
I can see them clearly
Because I don't get caught in them
In my fear
Or my shame
Or my loneliness
Or
My guilt
Or
My anger
Or
My hurt
I take things piece at a time
And I open up to this or that
I see it for what it is
I don't feel lost
I don't feel confused
Each thing becomes apparent
It is not muddled
I feel better about life
The it is better now

The Responsibility of Living or How Long Does This Go On

So, how long does this go on
It never stops
You mean I have to do this for ever
As long as you are
Do I have to
You cannot have it not go on
As long as you are
What if I do not want it to go on
Then you must not be
And that will be a going on then too
We all must be
Until we are not
Yet we must be to not be
There is no escaping it
The responsibility of living

Staccato

Sharp
Crisp
The movement of the therapeutic dialogue
Driven by the struggles
Brief responses
To the point
Seeking resolution
Moving on
Landing lightly on the moment
Seeing what drives the struggle
Asking simply

Pontification

Tell the client
And
He learns nothing
Ask the client
And
He will learn everything

Part IV:
Approaches to Therapy

Photo by Eadie Elliott

DSM

The Joke Book
A lot of names
Each conceived by vote
Sometimes timely to have a name sometimes not
We present the names like a sentence
We withdraw the names when we find no crime
It is a political game
We pretend we know something
When it has a name
Syndrome
With no etiology
Accusation
Without cause
With observed instances
You old name caller you

Patient Client

The patient is ill
The patient has a disease
The patient needs treatment
The patient is a passive agent
The client is not ill
The client has no disease
The client needs no treatment
The client is an active agent
In therapy
To medicalize is to distort
To distort is to confuse
To confuse is to make a mess
Look at the mess we have made

Doing Therapy with Yourself

Never believe you are doing so much
Never believe you know what is going on
Never believe you can fix anything
Never believe there is anything needing fixing
Never believe you know what the client does not
Never believe you are the agent of change
Never believe you can figure out the life of the client
Never believe you are ahead of the client
Never believe you are sooooo good
Never believe that what you think the client believes is what the client believe
Never believe you are in charge
Never believe your construction over the clients
Never do therapy with yourself
Listen to yourself
Your interpretation of the client
And not the client
And you will be doing therapy with yourself

Follow the Client

What did he say
Not what did you make of it
Not what you think about it
Not what it means to you
Not your explanation
What were *his* words
How did he put it
For certain not your interpretation
Ask him
What did He mean by what he said
What does He understand it to mean
When he doesn't know inquire about that
Never tell
Always ask
Sometimes you can ask "what about this" questions
But be careful
They need to come from Him
Not from you as if you were he
Follow the client

How do You Come to That

If I ask you WHY
I ask you to deny
I ask you to be defensive
I ask you to explain
I ask you to be confrontive
I ask you to justify
If I ask you *how*
I ask you to look at you
I ask you to see your movement
I ask you to report the steps you took
I ask you to look within
I ask you to understand you
I ask you to express how you be
I ask you to express the unexpressed
How do you come to that
Not why

Therapy is Mundane

Never the same problems
Always the same moves
Time after time
Always different
A little twist here
A little change there
Never the same
Always a little different
Therefore brand new
Never the same moves
Universes apart
Yet so close
How magnificent

Part V: Change

Photo by Eadie Elliott

What is Wrong with Me

I must be crazy
Crazy How
I don't see crazy
I must be sick
Sick How
I don't see sick
Well then I must be really stupid
Stupid how
I don't see stupid
Then I must just be an idiot
Idiot how
I don't see idiot
Well maybe I am just confused
Yes, confused
How
About what matters
And what matters
Well, I do and my children do
Hey, now I am getting somewhere
I think I get the idea

Therapy is About Change

Change comes from desire to be different
Change comes from effort
Change comes from action to alter
Altering
Change comes slowly
Through seeing differently
A hard job
We want to hold on to what we
See
Feel
Believe
Do
We want to be as we are
Not as we are not
Change comes from pain
If I hurt enough
Try enough
I may become other than I am
That I do not want to be
And become more what I wish to be

Seeing

When you look what do you see
Do you see yourself seeing
Or do you see beyond yourself
Do you see without self
Do you see selfless
Do you see for the first time
Do you see all seeing
Do you see
And what do you see when you see
Do you see birth
In every moment of sight another birth
Praise seeing the birth
And seeing that seeing is the birth of what is seen
Seeing is as full as your greatest dream
Love to see
Love seeing
Love being in the moment of seeing

Part VI: Self

Photo by Eadie Elliott

Hope

There is no hope
Is it okay if I smoke
It's dark tonight
Did you have a long day
I had an affair
So what has been going on with you
Nothing different
So everything is just the same as when we last met
Well, not... not exactly.
I'm cold
Can we go in
What is different from the last time we met
I see how I screw up
How is that
I get caught
How
I get to thinking the same crap
So, is it the thinking that gets you there
Well, yes
And where is there
I screw up
So thinking the same crap leads to screwing up
Yes
Can you quit that thinking
Yes, but...
But what
It would be hard
Yes

I Am

When do I find me
When I am open
When I no longer fear
When I am ready
When I can see
The I has always been
Has never been lost
I have only created a haze around I
I can remove it
I can see clearly
I can
I can see
I can see clearly
Clearly I can see
The haze is made of not looking
Not seeing
Not hearing
Not listening
Not being
I am

Understand

Understand
I do not understand:
I hurt
I am in pain
I am alone
I am suffering
I am in torment
I understand:
I do not hurt
I am not in pain
I am not alone
I am not suffering
I am not in torment
Conflict internal:
Do I trust me
Do I doubt me
Do I listen to me
I make up stories about me:
What I could have been
What I might have been
What I want to have been
What I am afraid to be
Better for me to resolve the conflict, stop the stories and understand

The Things I Don't Like

I don't like not knowing
Then seek to understand
I don't like to be wrong
Then do not act
I don't like being angry
Then do not contend
I do not like being alone
Then seek yourself
I do not like me
Then discover your soul
Be open to life
It will envelop you with happiness
Within

In the Name of Now

Not what I was
Not what I will be
What I am
What is now
What I am now
Now is I
I is present
Look and see
Where is I
I is here
I is now
I is me
I am
I

Happy

I want you to be happy
You want me to be happy
We want each other to be happy
If you are not happy
I am not happy
If I am not happy you are not happy
I will be happy
If you will be happy
Will you be happy if I am happy
You go first
I am afraid
I am afraid too
Together afraid
We will not be happy
We will not be together
We will not be
We will not
Let us be
And we will be happy
Happy we
Thank you again R.D. Laing

Fears

We all have our fears
Things we do not want to see
That is just the way it is
To be human
So
Look inside
You will see the fiction
You will see there is nothing
You will see there
As you see
The fears gone
Gone the fears
They were a figment
They were empty
I just needed to see how I built the vision
My vision
My creation
A thing done
A thing over
A thing seen through
A thing I no longer do to me

Everything Me

Everything that goes wrong comes from within me
I am the cause of all the bad things
Or is it just that I think it is like this
Well, what is the difference between thinking and doing
One is an idea
The other is an outward action
So
Are you having an idea
Or an outward action
An idea
Then no action
No
Then not the cause
No
Idea come from within
Yes
Within feel comes
Action not comes
Yes
Idea comes and Feeling comes
That is better

I Am the One I Seek

I seek my voice
I want to hear me
I want to speak
I want to be
I want
I want to know me
I want me to be here
I am the one I seek

My Safe Place

This is my safe place
I have never had a safe place before
Where I could tell someone anything
Where I was not afraid
Where I could be free
To think out loud
To open my mind
You are my friend
Truly my friend
I feel safe here
Oh, you have no idea
How safe I feel
Safe

Part VII: Relationship

Photo by Eadie Elliott

If You Let Them Go

If you let them go they will just keep on bickering
You have to stop them
You have to get them to take their moves apart
They have to see themselves acting
They have to find out what drives the trouble within
You must do this slowly
Point by point
Step by step
Word by word
Fear by fear
Shame by shame
Frustration by frustration
Confusion by confusion
Contradiction by contradiction
Uncertainty by uncertainty
Always by invitation
This is the process
The outcome is resolution

It is Difficult for Us

It is difficult
I am not sure how
It just comes to be that way
I don't know what the it even is
I know how it feels
Sluggish or caught
Trapped
Ashamed
Uncertain
God knows I know the trio:
Confusions, contradictions and uncertainties
But never on a personal basis before
Always in others
So many others
How I loved them all
How I miss them
Or it
Or us
Yes, us
Whatever happened to us for me
Can we find us again
I really want to

What is Going On

She said he never listens
He said she is always nagging
Yes, but what is happening
Listen nag
Nag listen
He feels criticized
She feels not heard
Good
So what is happening
She wants him to be more involved
He wants to feel loved by her
Not quite
He wants to feel accepted
She wants to feel understood
There it is

It's All About Me

So it's all about me
What's my problem
It's always you
You start it
I'm worthless
You're perfect
Perfect little thing
You bitch
You think I don't know
You think I don't know you're trying to get me
You think I'm paranoid
Well, let me tell you
I am suspicious for a good reason
I saw the way that guy looked at you
You egged him on
You did this to me
To me
You
It's not all about me
Is it

He Used to Love Me

He used to love me
I used to love him
I think I still love him
I say I do
I don't love what he does
Does he still love me
I think he does
He says he does
But he is with another woman
Will I ever let go
Do I want to let go
What will happen if I let go
Can I hold on
Is it possible
Is there anything to hold to
Yes
Me

Don't You Understand

Don't you understand
You are always telling me how to be
I never tell you how to be
You always do
I never do
Yes you do
No I don't
You just don't know it
But you do
You just think I do
And I never do
I just want you to be happy
No you don't
Yes I do
I love you
I don't feel loved

A Common Claim

Why do you always do that to me
Why do you make me be the way I don't want to be
Why do you hurt me that way
How dare you
You should be ashamed
Don't you love me
What have I done wrong
I don't deserve this
You are a monster
I have created you in my own mind
I am the author
You but the actor
My doing
Not yours

Part VIII:
Being Okay

Photo by Eadie Elliott

Crazy

Am I crazy
I don't know
But you're the doctor
You are supposed to know
I know
But I don't know
Do you know
Well I don't think I am
Well, then, that settles it
You are not crazy
How do you know
You told me
So
So now I know

Empty of Hurt

It Hurt
The more I looked the less I saw
I couldn't find me
I was hidden
I was lost
I was absent
I was not there
I was empty
I was alone
Then I waited
There I was
I found me in silence
I found me in patience
I found me in calm
The longer I waited
The more I worked
The more I saw
I was not alone
I was not empty
I was full
I was filled with everything
No more hurt

Incomplete

I am complete (done) when
I am complete when I quit
I am complete when I stop trying
I am complete when I blame
I am complete when I give in
I am complete when I know all
I am incomplete when
I am incomplete when I don't quit
I am incomplete when I try
I am incomplete when I do not blame
I am incomplete when I do not give in
I am incomplete when I can know more
Give me incompleteness

The End of Therapy

When shall we part
When will my therapy be over
When you say so
When you are done with this part of the doing
When you no longer need to come
When you do what we do
Without me there
When you do
What you do here
Without thinking about doing it
When all this becomes a way, a style, a pattern and a standard of living
Then you will be through
Through that much
Then nothing will be any different thereafter
You will continue to grow
You will continue
You will
You
Will

Part IX:
The Therapist

Photo by Eadie Elliott

In the First Years of the Therapist

What to ask
Where to begin
There is so much
Which part is important
There is so little
To be sure of what to pursue
Over the years
There are so many important disclosures
It becomes a matter of priorities
Which parts of all the things to examine first
To take each
In its turn
To forget none
To open each matter
To examine the question's question
To wait
To listen
To be still
Be the mirror
Which reflects
The innuendo

Time for Therapy

The easiest of cases
Not much at all to this one
Lasts for years
And ends poorly
The hardest of cases
This life is a total shambles
Lasts only for a few months
And ends well
No telling the time for therapy

Therapy Timeout

The client comes in
Begins to reflect
Takes a break from the day to day world
Almost like play
Though for the therapist
Mundane
Routine
Labor of love
For the patient
Almost play
A toying with
A teasing
A trying on new cloths
A looking in the mirror
Dress up
And then the beauty
I have become
The product of my play
For I now know
My play has revealed me to me
I am alive in the best of ways
I am open
I am free
I am responsible

Stillness

Be patient
Be still
All else is hustle and bustle
All else is contradiction
Move as the stars
Move as the moon
Be awake to your quiet
See yourself in slow motion
Be slow motion
Move as the turtle
Be free from hurry
Be free from over abundant anticipation
Be free from wasted motion
Be patient
Be still
Be free
As you are meant to be
Thank you for teaching me patience my patients my mentor
And thank you Paul

Mentor

So, he would say
Can you see it now
Then turn it around
Look at it from the other side.
Can you see what is happening now
I don't want to know what you think
I want to know what she said
How did she put it
Follow him
Where is he going
What is missing
What is not there
You will see it
Just look

Turn It Around

Look at it from the other way
He would say
What else might it be
He would say
Can you see it differently
He would say
What else is there
He would say
You're missing something
He would say
He would say
Turn it around
So often
It turned out
The way he turned it around
Experience
Teaches
Teachers
Experience
Enough years looking
And you begin
To see the way it turns

Trust the Doctor

Trust me I am a Doctor
This is how you should be
This is what you should be
This is when you should be
This is why you should be
This is where you should be
Be this
Above all
Mistrust this doctor

Terminations

I've been thinking
I think I don't need to come to therapy any more
I've been thinking that too
Is it okay if I give you a call once in a while
Yes, I look forward to our conversations
I am not going anywhere
I will be here
I will look forward to your calls

So

So after thirty years of being a therapist
What have you learned
To be quiet
No
I mean really learned
To be curious
No
You know what I mean
Oh,
You mean like to be quietly curious
Or
I learned to follow people
To go where they go
Only then can I know who
They have been and are becoming
I have learned how to know
What I am told
It is sort of like knowing
What you haven't known
Knowing it is not your knowing
When you do know
It is just knowing following
And then knowing from the following

In a Flash

You can be there in a flash
Where your client is
Hurting
In pain
Your whole life a mess
You can be where your client is
In a Flash
Never think otherwise
Do not think you are above it
Do not think you are free of the risk
Of developing a horrid
Way, style and pattern of living
It is a slippery slope
Only seen after words
Never before

Me

Me I know I don't know
I do not presume to know
I try not to presume at all
I work at being open
Thus I often appear to be working more than to be being open
I also work at loving
This is very difficult
For I am judgmental
In the sense of being critical
In the sense of holding everything I discern
Up to a criteria
I want to know what, how, why, when, where, who
And all other things related…
How often, why not, under what conditions
And all the rest
I detest judgment
As discerning
The worth or value of a person
It's just prejudice
In all that I don't know I am prejudice
I am working on changing that to
A life's work and more

Part X:
Outcomes

Photo by Eadie Elliott

If I Go Forward What

And if I go forward what
Well then you will not be here
You will be elsewhere
And will it be any better
What would be better
If I were not so ashamed
So, you just saw better there
I see what if
I kinda see the how
I do see that there is not here
I see the possibility of change
I do see that
Have I begun to change
You have gone forward
That is change

Change

I don't want to change
Let go of me
I don't want to
I don't have to
I won't
I can't
Why should I
When did I learn to start and not to quit
Embrace me
Let's do
I want to
I will
I can
Because I will
I have changed
I am change
I will to change
Changed
I love change

Moment

Be well with yourself and others
Find your moment
It belongs to you
Share it with others
They will cherish it forever
Be still and listen
You will hear the essence of life
As you reach out
So you will be reached for
Give
Though remember to receive
Be calm
Yet know what energy you have
Above all things peace and love
Seek these for they are wondrous and resolve all suffering

Present or Hi

I still see my therapist
Now and again on the street or in a shop
I say hey hi
I remember when I could not think well
Without him being present
Now I can do with me what I did with him
I can question the things that are mixed up
I can see their parts clearly bit at a time
I learn more about me at each look
I begin to see the whole
I begin to see what is there
The distortion clears
I am present for me

Empty of Hurt

It hurt
The more I looked the less I saw
I couldn't find me
I was hidden
I was lost
I was absent
I was not there
I was empty
I was alone
Then I waited
There I was
I found me in silence
I found me in patience
I found me in calm
The longer I waited
The more I worked
The more I saw
I was not alone
I was not empty
I was full
I was filled with everything
No more hurt

It Seen or the It of Things

The it of things
Usually hidden
Seldom seen
Not it is a mess
But
What a mess I have gotten myself into
Here not hidden
Here seen
It seen
Seeing it
Seeing
The it of things is finally seen

Mostly the Words Play

When the sessions go well
They are less work and more play
A bantering among themselves
The words go on
Effortlessly
Without any trying
One idea
Jumps off the next
The two come together
They blend and make sense
Then the next idea emerges
It fits too
It is as though I do not have to try
I simply see more of what was hidden
Simply I see more
I see simply
Without seeming
Just being
Flowing
Listening
Understanding

I Can

I can say it freely
That is,
I can explore
I can be confused out loud
It can be okay
I can not know what "it" is
I can be unsure
It is so freeing
I don't have to know
Yet, not knowing
I begin to see
I see it
It is the uncertainty
It is the confusion
It is the contradiction
Actually it is me
The way I see things
The way I live
I can see that I did not see
I see how to see
So refreshing

The Waterfall

The waterfall
As in all things
Comes to rest
You have seen the movement
The movement has been with you
In part you have become the change
In part you have been the change
In part you know the change
In part you are still now
In part you have changed
In part you are not as you were
In part you have grown
You have not arrived
The journey is you
The journey is within you
Until the next
Waterfall
The journey
continues

www.ingramcontent.com/pod-product-compliance
Lightning Source LLC
Chambersburg PA
CBHW070542170426
43200CB00011B/2525